Elevate Your Career

The Friend-Influence Blueprint

Nora S. Radley

Table Of Content

Introduction

In the unique scene of the present proficient world, where each cooperation holds the possibility to be a venturing stone towards significance, "Raise Your Profession: The Companion Impact Diagram" remains a reference point of edification. It is a tribute to the significant effect that human associations can use, reverberating long past the bounds of meeting rooms and workspaces.

Inside these pages, you will set out on a groundbreaking endeavor, revealing the complexities of relationship construction that reach a long way past the spur-of-the-moment trade of business cards. This is an excursion through the actual quintessence of human association, a journey to the core of certifiable, enduring impact.

Digging profoundly into the archives of brain research, social science, and genuine encounters, this book rises above the superficial thoughts of systems administration. It enlightens the craft of understanding, sympathizing, and teaming up with people who share your vision and enthusiasm. It provokes you to perceive that the force of your organization is not a simple device, but an important resource that can be sharpened and utilized for unrivaled development.

In "Raise Your Profession," you will experience stories of pioneers who, furnished with the insight of significant associations, have risen above regular vocation directions to make a permanent imprint on their ventures. Their accounts act as a demonstration of the significant truth that it's what you know, yet who you know and, all the more critically, how you draw in with them.

Plan to rethink your way of dealing with proficient connections, for inside these sections lies the way to opening a domain where your impact stretches out a long way past the bounds of your work title. This is an encouragement to develop an organization that isn't simply far-reaching, yet persevering — established in credibility, reason, and shared values.

As you retain the insight held inside these pages, you will arise not just outfitted with the instruments to explore the complicated dance of expert associations, but additionally with a newly discovered appreciation for the groundbreakilikelihoodely that exists in each relationship, ready to be lighted.

Thus, dear peruser, leave on this excursion with an open heart and an eager brain, for the Companion Impact Outline isn't simply a procedure — a way of thinking can reshape the actual texture of your profession. This is your encouragement to rise higher than ever, directed by the force of genuine human associations. Your process is standing by.

Chapter 1

Getting a handle on Your Profession Process

In the dynamic and continually changing proficient climate of today, beginning a vocation without an unmistakable objective is tantamount to cruising without a compass. It is difficult to stretch the significance of key professional arranging; it is the guide that leads you through the diversions and guarantees you show up at your objective with aim and reason.

Vital Vocation Arranging: It's Worth

See yourself as at a mountain's foot. You have a decision: arm yourself with a very much arranged course, supplies, and a reasonable vision of the pinnacle, or climb heedlessly and desire to arrive at the culmination. Like this, essential vocation arranging gives you the information and capacities needed to arrange the difficulties of your picked calling. You gain the capacity to pursue choices that are by your longings, spot open doors, and put forth critical objectives.

A Changing Climate for Occupation Market Transformation

The work market of today is different from that of the past. Versatility has arisen as a critical component of progress because of globalization, mechanical upgrades, and moving modern elements. Being gifted alone isn't sufficient; you likewise should be versatile, open to new doors, and deft. The strategies and mentalities analyzed in this part are critical for prevailing in this powerful, always changing workplace.

Enduring Change as a Chance for Advancement

The cutting-edge work market consistently shapes and reshapes professional pathways, similar to what a waterway does with the scene it goes through. It's simpler to get new encounters, ranges of abilities, and possibilities for development when you embrace change as opposed to opposing it. We'll show you how being proactive about change can prod both your own and proficient turn of events.

Making Your Singular Profession Story

Your vocation is something beyond an assortment of occupations; a story lays out your healthy identity as a laborer. You have the potential chance to make a story that epitomizes your qualities, interests, and objectives through cautious preparation and flexibility. This segment offers supportive counsel on the most proficient method to possess your professional account and change it with the goal that from requests to both you and your crowd.

Remember that your profession is a material ready to be painted with reason and vision as we set out on this experience together. You get the opportunity to explore your course and make a critical commitment to the expert climate through essential readiness and an unmistakable handle of the changing work market. We should begin down the way to a calling propelled by reason.

Chapter 2

Grasping Human Way of behaving: The Underpinning of Profound Connections

Each expert contact rotates upon the mind-boggling dance of the human way of behaving. Veritable grins that set others straight, smart activities that show sympathy, and giggling shared by gatherings all add to the development of ties. Producing associations that reverberate on a more profound level requires a comprehension and enthusiasm for these nuances.

The Ensemble of Feelings in Work Environment Conditions

Envision a bustling office, with the fulfillment of an unparalleled piece of handiwork, the uneasiness of a cutoff time drawing closer, and the harmony during a group festivity. A top-to-bottom assessment of the feelings that influence our expert connections and direction is given in this part.

The underpinning of a genuine association is sympathy.

Envision encountering the preliminaries and triumphs of another person. The underpinning of satisfying connections is sympathy, which empowers us to associate profoundly with others. We'll look at how you could create and impart sympathy in your vocation through practical stories and helpful activities.

Nonverbal Signs: A Dance

Ponder the nonverbal prompts we as a whole use to impart: areas of strength for the, the consoling gesture of congratulations, the vigilant gesture. This part makes sense of the unpretentious signs that underlie our conversations so you can figure out them and respond to them deftly.

Being available and tuning in with aim

Recollect when somebody pays attention to you without interference or inclination. Providing others with the endowment of undivided attention shows them that we appreciate and esteem their perspectives. We'll sharpen your ability to be thoroughly present in each discussion with vivid exercises and genuine biographies.

Consider the events when you and your guides have been nearer: a success on a joint venture, a diversion you both appreciate beyond work, or even a typical impediment you defeated together. The strength of shared encounters in fortifying proficient associations is praised in this part.

Remember that behind each title, each capability, and each leader is an individual with expectations, concerns, and goals as we start this examination concerning the human way of behaving. You can make authentic, dependable associations in your expert life by fathoming and embracing the lavishness of human contact.

Chapter 3

Self-Evaluation and Objective Setting:

Exploring Your Profession Way with Clearness and Reason

Leaving on an effective vocation venture is much the same as heading out on a journey of self-revelation and expert development. This part is committed to the reflective course of figuring out oneself, perceiving qualities, recognizing shortcomings, and graphing a course toward a future loaded with reason and satisfaction.

Recognizing Your Assets and Shortcomings: Embracing Your Extraordinary Embroidery

Envision a nursery, each blossom unmistakable in its tone, shape, and scent. Essentially, you are a mosaic of qualities and regions for development. Through thoughtfulness and genuine self-reflection, you'll uncover the features of your character, abilities, and gifts that put you aside. We'll praise your assets, saddling them as your signal, while likewise recognizing your regions for improvement with sympathy and a pledge to development.

For example, consider when your assets sparkled splendidly, enlightening a venture or a group. Think about minutes when you confronted difficulties, and how those encounters formed your assurance to improve and develop.

Characterizing Clear Profession Goals: Portraying the Plan of Your Desires

Picture your optimal expert scene. Which jobs do you imagine? What effect do you seek to make? Through a smart course of imagining, you'll explain your professional targets. We'll dig into your desires, from transient achievements to long-haul dreams, and blueprint significant stages to overcome any barrier between where you are presently and where you need to be.

Consider the fulfillment you'll get from accomplishing these objectives - regarding proficient achievement, yet in addition to the individual satisfaction that comes from adjusting your vocation to your interests and values.

Embracing the Excursion of Development: Your Vocation Story Unfurls

Your vocation is not a static objective, but a unique story that develops over the long haul. This segment urges you to see your excursion as a continuous story of development and learning. Embrace the difficulties, misfortunes, and wins as sections that shape the account of your profession.

Contemplate the tales you'll tell, the abilities you'll gain, and the effect you'll make en route. Envision the snapshots of development and change that will improve your expert process.

Making a Steady Biological system: Developing Connections and Assets

Similarly, as a tree flourishes in prolific soil, your profession thrives in a sustaining climate. This part investigates the significance of building an organization of tutors, partners, and assets that engage your development. We'll examine how to look for direction, offer help, and team up with others on your common process towards progress.

Envision the association you'll create, the mentors who will offer courses, and the associations that will offer extremely valuable assistance as you investigate your calling way.

Toward the finish of this segment, you'll have set out on a groundbreaking excursion of self-disclosure and objective setting. With a reasonable comprehension of your assets, yearnings, and the means should have tried to understand them, you'll be ready to explore your profession with a newly discovered feeling of clearness and reason. Together, we should set out on this journey of self-revelation and expert development, graphing a course toward a ture loaded with satisfaction and achievement.

Chapter 4

Making Your Expert Character: Painting Your Novel Material in the Expert World

Similarly, as a craftsman chooses their range with care, you also can shape the account of your expert character. This part is material for you to communicate your gifts, values, and desires, permitting you to hang out in the cutthroat scene of your picked field.

Building an Individual Brand for Profession Achievement: Your Embodiment in Each Connection

Your image is the engraving you leave on the expert world, the substance that partners and colleagues partner with you. Consider it the handshake that waits long after the gathering is finished. Through a mix of credibility and purposefulness, we'll investigate how you can shape an individual brand that mirrors your assets as well as reverberates with your qualities.

Consider the effect you need to make, the qualities you hold dear, and the characteristics you need to be known for. Imagine how your image will have an enduring effect on those you experience in your expert process.

Making a Significant Resume and LinkedIn Profile: Your Story, Your Way

Envision your resume and LinkedIn profile as parts of the tale of your vocation. They are the initial look into your expert process that expected businesses and associates experience. Together, we'll make a story that catches your abilities and encounters, yet additionally, the energy and reason that drive you.

Picture the words that will jump off the page, exhibiting your accomplishments, your commitment, and the extraordinary point of view you bring. Imagine how your profile will welcome others to interface with the credible, driven proficient that you are.

Winding around Your Expert Account: Adjusting Your Story to Your Objectives

Your vocation isn't a progression of separated occasions, but a story that unfurls with reason. This part urges you to see your encounters, the two victories and difficulties, as strings that wind around together the embroidery of your expert character. Through insightful reflection, we'll adjust your account to your yearnings, making a story that resounds with credibility and vision.

Envision the cohesiveness and power that will radiate from a profession story that is intentionally created to mirror your excursion, values, and desires.

Exemplifying Your Expert Personality: From Words to Activities

Your expert personality isn't bound to a piece of paper or a computerized profile; it is exemplified in each cooperation, each choice, and each undertaking. This segment investigates how you can experience your expert image genuinely, adjusting your activities to the character you've made.

Imagine the effect of living in coinciding with your expert personality - the trust you'll fabricate, the connections you'll support, and the valuable open doors that will normally float towards you.

By the finish of this part, you will have characterized your expert way of life as well as encapsulated it with expectation and realness. Together, we'll make a story that addresses what your identity is, a big motivator for you, and the effect you're ready to make in the expert world. We should progress forward with this excursion of self-articulation and deliberate personality making, painting a material that is interestingly, proudly you.

Chapter 5

Dominating Quest for new employment Systems: Clearing Your Way to Proficient Satisfaction

Setting out on a pursuit of employment isn't just about tracking down a job; about finding an open door that lines up with your goals and values. This part is a compass, directing you through successful procedures and systems administration methodologies that go past the surface, it is deliberate and compensating to guarantee your excursion.

Viable Pursuit of employment Methods: Past Catchphrases and Channels

Worksheets and web indexes are only a hint of something larger. This segment digs into the specialty of a nuanced quest for new employment, where distinguishing the perfect open doors is a fine art. We'll investigate how to reveal unlikely treasures, target organizations that reverberate with your qualities, and specialty applications that hang out in an ocean of resumes.

Organizing for Open positions: Building Scaffolds, Making Prospects

Organizing is more than a conditional trade of business cards; developing certified connections can be the impetus for new open doors. We'll dig into the craft of significant systems administration, from going to occasions with reason to cultivating associations that reach out past the surface.

Envision the entryways that will open when you approach organizing with legitimacy and a certified interest in others. Imagine the mentorships, joint efforts, and open doors that will rise out of these authentic associations.

Utilizing On the web Stages: From LinkedIn to Industry Gatherings

In the present advanced age, online stages have become virtual commercial centers for work searchers and managers the same. This part gives down-to-earth bits of knowledge on the most proficient method to enhance your web-based presence, from making a champion LinkedIn profile to taking part in industry-explicit gatherings where valuable open doors frequently surface.

Picture your online presence as a magnet for open entryways, drawing in enlistment trained professionals and partners who are restless to communicate with the gifted master you are.

Exploring Position Fairs and Systems administration Occasions: From Contacts to Associations

Work fairs and systems administration occasions are not just about gathering business cards; they're tied in with establishing critical connections and laying out associations that can prompt future joint efforts. We'll investigate procedures for capitalizing on these occasions, from moving toward discussions with reason to following up such that makes way for continuous connections.

Imagine yourself as a certain, congenial expert who has an enduring impact on each individual you experience on these occasions.

Toward the finish of this part, you'll have a complete toolbox for a pursuit of employment that goes past superficial applications. Through viable methods and certifiable systems administration, you'll be ready to reveal amazing open doors that line up with your goals and values. We should leave on this excursion of intentional pursuit of employment, where each step carries you more like a job that satisfies and energizes you.

Chapter 6

Acing Meetings and Establishing Enduring Connections:

Displaying Your Exceptional Brightness in Each Experience

...A meeting isn't simply a gathering; it's an opportunity to interface, to share your story, and to check whether your potential future lines up with the organization's vision. This part is your manual for getting ready for interviews, yet venturing into every cooperation with realness, certainty, and a certified longing to contribute.

Planning for Meetings: Exploration and Practice

Envision going into a meeting room feeling like you as of now have a place. It's about something beyond knowing the organization's items or administrations; it's tied in with grasping their way of life, their difficulties, and what is most important to them. This part is tied in with submerging yourself in the organization's reality, so you can communicate in their language and resound with their objectives.

Picture the effect you'll make when you figure out the organization's main goal, yet in addition, consider yourself to be an essential piece of acknowledging it.

Exploring Social Meetings and Evaluations: Disclosing Your Actual Potential

,...Interviews aren't just about abilities; they're about your thought process, how you approach issues, and how you work together. This segment is your chance to sparkle, to share accounts of difficulties you've confronted, and to show how you've transformed them into wins. It's tied in with being more than a resume; it's tied in with being your very own narrator process.

Imagine the association you'll make when you share your achievements, yet the substance behind them.

Dominating Non-Verbal Correspondence: The Dance of Association

,..Your presence in a meeting says a lot. It's how you hold yourself, the radiance in your eyes, and the glow of your grin. This segment is tied in with being available, about radiating certainty and congeniality, and about making an association that goes beyond anything that can be described.

Envision the energy you'll bring into the room, causing everybody you meet to feel like they've recently met somebody unique.

Resolving Extreme Inquiries with Beauty and Credibility

Extreme inquiries aren't simply tests; they're solicitations to share your excursion, your development, and your flexibility. This segment is tied in with embracing these minutes, about transforming weaknesses into qualities, and about showing that you're ready for the gig, yet for the difficulties that accompany it.

Imagine the trust you'll fabricate when you talk from the heart, tending to difficulties with an insight that comes as a matter of fact.

The Craft of Following Up: Having an Enduring Impression

The discussion doesn't end with a handshake and a grin; it goes on in the development. This segment is tied in with offering your thanks, repeating your energy, and showing that you're searching for a task, yet for a spot where you can contribute and develop.

Picture the effect of an earnest development, reminding them for what reason you're another up-and-comer, however, somebody who could be an important colleague.

Toward the finish of this part, you won't only be prepared for interviews; you'll be prepared to interface, to share, and to have an enduring impression. With every collaboration, you'll bring a piece of your real self, showing that you're searching for a task, however for a chance to carry your splendor to a group that will genuinely esteem it. We should leave on this excursion together, where each experience is an opportunity to hit one out of the ballpark and make a significant association.

Chapter 7

Executing Standards: Connecting Hypothesis to Useful Application

The way to authority includes something other than knowing; it likewise includes activity. This segment is your viable guidance manual and is expected to interpret thoughts into substantial activities and capacities. You will learn subjects through involved exercises, practical circumstances, and vivid encounters, incorporating them so they become a characteristic piece of your expert toolbox.

Taking Information and Trying It: Significant Stages for Surefire Execution

Envision having the keys to making the way for genuine outcomes in your grasp. Your getting the keys is the focal point of this part. We'll turn troublesome thoughts into feasible advances that you can begin utilizing immediately. You'll find commonsense bits of knowledge that furnish you to manage the challenges of the expert world, from productive specialized strategies to time usage strategies.

Envision the confirmation you would feel if you knew what to do, yet in addition how to achieve it such that it felt certifiable and proficient to you.

Creating Expertise Through Activities and Situations: Inserting Authority

Working on, investing the effort, and submerging yourself in genuine circumstances is how dominance is accomplished. This part is your training region, with errands that reflect the challenges you'll experience in your profession. In a protected and empowering setting, you'll get the opportunity to clean your gifts through pretending circumstances and critical thinking difficulties.

As you approach these exercises with devotion and receptiveness to learning, picture the development that will happen.

Smart Journaling: Propelling Personal Development and Care

Reflection is the compass that guides you as you travel on your way to capable power. This part asks you to keep a wise diary in which you can record your discernment, screen your new development, and perceive your accomplishments. It's a spot for you to learn about yourself, perceive your abilities, and pinpoint potential improvement districts.

Consider the profundity of mindfulness and self-improvement that will result from this thoughtful and intelligent activity.

Circles of friend learning and criticism: cultivating a local area of improvement

You are a piece of a local area of students who are going various ways to dominance, so you are not voyaging this outing alone. The counsel in this part is to make peer learning and criticism bunches so you might help and gain from each other. It fills in as a discussion for trading stories, giving supportive analysis, and complimenting each other on achievements.

Imagine the strength of each other assembling and are on a comparable method for advancing.

Concerning: Seeing Your Success and Achievements

You will encounter both basic and minor vital turning points en route to strength. This locale engages you to see the worth in your turn of events and compliment your accomplishments as well as your progression. It fills in as a period for thought and appreciation, an indication of your progression to date the normal that remains before you.

Envision the energy of pride and accomplishment that will go with each accomplishment, awakening you to keep on pushing ahead on this method of headway.

You won't just have data ensuing to examine this part; you'll live it. You will absorb the considerations and limits expected for progress in the workplace through rehearses that are both valuable and canny, assessment, peer learning, and merriment. Together, we'll consolidate speculation and make thoughts customized. We ought to start this valuable outing of progress and predominance, where each step is a phase toward transforming into the expert you should be.

Chapter 8

Congruity in an Embroidery of Variety:

Encouraging Transformation to Different Characters

You'll go over many characters in the feverish work environment, each adding their unmistakable note to the orchestra of your expert turn of events. This part centers around esteeming contrasts, finding areas of understanding, and making spans that sound valid and identify with others.

Working with Individuals of Various Characters: The Dance of Understanding

Envision a group where every individual brings a one-of-a-kind arrangement of abilities, experiences, and procedures to bear on issues. This part talks about flourishing in this powerful nature as opposed to just making due there. It's tied in with perceiving the worth of variety and valuing the allure of how even assorted characters cooperate.

Envision the synchronicity that happens when every part's unmistakable capacities consolidate to make an aggregate splendor that progresses the group.

Capitalizing on Your Methodology: An Orchestra of Associations

You can tweak your way to deal with reverberate with every individual you come into contact with, similarly as a performer picks the best instrument for each piece. Purposeful tuning in, empathic perception, and altering your correspondence style to meet individuals where they are completely shrouded in this part.

Envision the strength of a relationship created by true sympathy and status to meet individuals where they are.

Overseeing Clashes Smoothly and Delicately

Struggle isn't a hindrance; rather, it is an opportunity for improvement and more noteworthy comprehension. This segment examines how to deal with conflicts with a receptive outlook and heart. About finding arrangements regarding the prerequisites and perspectives of every interested individual and pushing ahead along a course that joins instead of partitions.

Envision the trust that would develop after individuals understand your devotion to settling debates in an empathetic and evenhanded way.

Making Extensions for Joint Effort and Trust

Each viable group is shaped based on trust. In this part, we'll discuss creating connections that go past titles and obligations in the working environment. It's vital to continually turn up, be reliable, and show that you're more than just a collaborator — you're an accomplice in their prosperity.

Envision the force of a gathering where trust is the strong string that joins them and drives them toward normal goals.

Embracing the Development Excursion Together

Your master outing isn't static; it is constantly creating, and people you meet in transit are your journeying mates. This area is connected to supporting each other as we learn and develop together, acclaim our triumphs, and beat obstacles. It incorporates understanding that you are significant for a neighborhood is trying to achieve a common goal, not just partners.

Imagine the friendship that will make as you come to this method of progress and exposure, lauding one another's triumphs and getting from one another's experiences.

You will not simply value arranged characters around the completion of this model, but you will in like manner regard them. You'll encourage affiliations that resonate with sincerity and compassion while investigating the difficulties of human contact with the class. Together, you'll convey a melodic ensemble that works on the spirit of your gathering along with the entire workplace. We ought to set out on this excursion of discernment, fulfillment, and improvement, where each character is a valued note in the demonstration of your master new development.

Chapter 9

Work-Life Amicability:

Advancing It in Your Expert Turn of Events

Becoming overpowered by the requests of work in the buzzing about of the expert world is straightforward. This part fills in as a delicate update that your well-being is the underpinning of a prosperous and compensating position. It's tied in with moving to the beat of a healthy lifestyle where work and individual satisfaction coincide in a delightful ensemble, not tied in with shuffling.

Focusing on Your Wellbeing in Your Vocation: The Way to Progress

Consider your well-being the compass that leads you through the wilderness of commitments and cutoff times. To make proficient progress, it is essential to deal with your physical, profound, and mental prosperity, which is the focal point of this part. We'll take a gander at possible taking care of oneself strategies, for example, care activities and creating healthy schedules that are great for your body and soul.

Envision the energy and relentlessness your expert process would have when you focus on your well-being as a pivotal part of your prosperity.

Communicating Yes to Yourself: The Specialty of Enduring Cutoff points

Limits aren't walls; rather, they're assurance for your time, energy, and soul. You are urged to lay out and maintain limits that safeguard your prosperity in this part. When to say "OK" to amazing open doors and when to say "OK" to oneself means a lot to be aware. We'll go over the long haul-the-board methods that will empower you to plan rest, work, and different exercises in a way that advances your general prosperity.

Envision the opportunity you will encounter once you understand that it isn't simply vital but additionally proper to put your requirements and wants first.

Building Huge Associations: Rearranging Work and Individual Associations.

Your expert process is connected to the texture of your own life; it doesn't exist alone. The connections that make your life significant, cheerful, and strong are what's truly going on with this part. It includes finding some kind of harmony between proficient commitments and investing energy with friends and family. We'll talk about how to work on your expert and individual associations through powerful correspondence, mindful tuning in, and the formation of significant encounters.

At the point when you put resources into the connections that are generally essential to you, simply consider the profundity of satisfaction and association that will infest your life.

The Force of Rest and Reflection for Revival and Recharging

For long-haul achievement and inventiveness, rest is a prerequisite, not an extravagance. This part urges you to acknowledge unwinding and thoughtfulness as crucial parts of your expert turn of events. It includes understanding that margin time isn't lost time but rather a time of recharging that helps your innovativeness and efficiency. We'll take a gander at procedures for loosening up, pondering oneself, and rehearsing care that will refuel your soul and reignite your energy.

Envision how alive and keen you will be at the point at which you are very much refreshed and resuscitated.

Noticing Achievements and Regarding Outcomes in the Two Universes

Achievement penetrates each component of your life; it isn't restricted to the expert world. This region stretches out a solicitation to you to honor both your expert and individual achievements that have given you joy and happiness. It includes tolerating that your prosperity and achievements in the two domains merit acknowledgment and festivity.

Imagine the vibes of accomplishment and appreciation that will go with each accomplishment, building up your conviction that you can win in both your master's and individual endeavors.

You'll not just have thoughts about shuffling work and life toward the finish of this section, but, you'll likewise have a new appreciation for the finesse of serene living. You might make a day-to-day existence that vibrates with satisfaction and significance by putting a need on your prosperity, defining limits, developing associations, and perceiving achievements. We should go out on this street of cultivating congruity together, where work and individual prosperity meet up in a beautiful, significant dance.

Chapter 10

Having Intense Discussions:

Managing Deterrents Actually and with Sympathy

There are times in the realm of expert cooperation when nuance, sympathy, and boldness are required. This part fills in as a manual for enduring specific minutes as opposed to just confronting them. Acknowledging provoking discussions are not boundaries to understanding, but rather venturing stones to more grounded associations.

Settling on something worth agreeing on and Beating Contrasts in Proficient Connections

Envision what is happening where clashes are seen as opportunities for improvement and more profound coordinated effort as opposed to obstacles. This part talks about how to determine debates agreeably and astutely. It's tied in with the understanding that different perspectives are not obstructions, but rather significant bits of the entirety. We'll go over approaches to effectively tune in, lay out marks of understanding, and search for arrangements that regard the necessities and stresses, everything being equal.

Envision the trust and regard that will develop because of settling debates with compassion, bringing about bonds that are not only fixed but supported.

Knowing Your Capacity to appreciate individuals on a profound level: The Way to Fruitful Discussions

Troublesome discussions include more than essential words; they additionally include sentiments. This part moves you to utilize your ability to appreciate people on a deeper level to explore your feelings with sympathy and empathy as well as those of others. We'll take a gander at strategies for recognizing and esteeming feelings, laying out a solid climate for sincere correspondence, and coming to choices that regard everybody's close-to-home prosperity.

Envision the degree of understanding and association that will emerge when sentiments act as extensions as opposed to deterrents in connections.

Giving productive analysis: Advancing Turn of events

Criticism is an interest in development; it goes past straightforward analysis. This part examines how to give criticism in a manner that energizes development and learning. It includes laying out an input circle because of certainty and a common devotion to improvement. We'll take a gander at ways of outlining analysis productively, give substantial models, and give thoughts for development that might be tried.

Consider how your ideas will be felt as they empower improvement and empower individuals to understand their most prominent potential.

Dynamic Critical Thinking: Collaboration Prompts Dependable Arrangements

Challenges that need arrangements now and again come up in troublesome discoursed. This part talks about how to move toward issues as opportunities for collaboration and advancement. It includes consolidating all gatherings in the quest for answers that arrange with the ongoing issue as well as laying the foundation for long-haul achievement. We'll take a gander at techniques for choosing thoughts and making activity arrangements that produce substantial results.

Envision the feeling of achievement and headway that will result from effectively partaking in conversational critical thinking.

Building Versatility and Trust: The Impacts of Extreme Discussions

A difficult discussion is best decided following it. The reason for this segment is to depict how to encourage trust and flexibility after troublesome discussions. It's tied in with demonstrating a craving to progress, acquiring information from the experience, and upgrading the association. We'll take a gander at ways of following up, keep the lines of correspondence open, and ensure the conversation brings about development and information.

Envision the profundity and strength of a relationship that gets through a troublesome talk more grounded, knowing that both of you defeated the obstruction, yet in addition, conquered it together.

When you wrap up perusing this part, you'll not exclusively be prepared to deal with testing talks, however, you'll likewise have the confidence to transform them into opportunities for self-awareness and closer connections. You'll beat deterrents with balance and viability by showing compassion, the capacity to understand people on a deeper level, and great correspondence. We should set off on this street to dominate awkward conversations, where each trade fills in as a springboard for building better, more sturdy connections in the working environment.

Chapter 11

Building a Durable and Satisfying Vocation:

Making an Energetic and Deliberate Proficient Pathway

Your calling is something past a quick overview of occupations; it's a tale about how you've changed, what you've contributed, and what that has meant for the world. This part is a veritable assessment of making a winding of encounters that mark cooperation with importance and satisfaction, not simply getting some work. Understanding that your calling is a fresh start simply maintaining a level of control for the brushstrokes of your single way is essential.

Adjusting Desire and Reason to Fabricate a Maintainable and Significant Vocation

Think about your expert life as a journey across a scene of choices, with every open door filling in as a venturing stone to an objective that is reliable with your qualities and goals. Making a course that isn't just aggressive yet in addition significantly significant is the focal point of this segment. About settling on choices that are following your actual self and picking objectives that address your heart. We'll go over how to foster a feeling of direction in each move you make, find open doors that fit with your qualities, and plan your profession out over the long haul.

Envision the fulfillment that will accompany every achievement, realizing that you are not just ascending the stepping stool but also rising to a spot that feels like home.

Flourishing in a Scene That Is Continuously Evolving: Embracing Development and Transformation

The workplace is dynamic and continually delivers new satisfaction. This part talks about flourishing despite change rather than only keeping up. It consolidates exploring through remarkable openings for coaching, limit advancement, and development as per business and industry systems. We'll take a gander at approaches for keeping up with status mindfulness, searching out clever communications, and involving change as an impetus for progression.

Envision the persistence and affirmation you will ooze as you arrange the high points and low points of your vocation process.

Cultivating Mentorship and Coordinated Effort: The Strength of Gathering Improvement

Your process is certainly not a single one; it is interlaced with that of the expert world. This segment is a source of inspiration to search for guides, accomplices, and similar people who can give guidance, backing, and intelligence. It's tied in with seeing that improvement is a collective dance of motivation and corresponding upliftment as opposed to just a singular action.

Imagine the significance of knowledge and the broadness of experiences that will result from the affiliations you make in transit all through your calling.

Leaving Your Imprint Beyond the Work Environment: Leaving a Positive Inheritance

Your calling is something other than whatever you achieve for yourself; it's likewise about the impression you make on the world. Perceiving your capability to impact positive change in both your expert climate and the bigger local area is the focal point of this part. Tracking down ways of coaching others, rewarding the local area, and leaving a tradition of liberality, genuineness, and critical commitment is extremely significant.

Envision the motivation and change that will spread from you, affecting your prompt proficient organizations as well as the bigger globe.

Observing Achievements: Perceiving Your Advancement and Achievement

There will be stones along your vocational way that remember your achievements as well as the general excursion. This segment is planned to act as a snapshot of reflection and festivity. Perceiving your turn of events, your endeavors, and the impact you've had on others around you is significant. It fills in as an update that each activity, regardless of how minuscule, exhibits your responsibility and perseverance.

When you wrap up perusing this part, you'll have a profession as well as a heritage that will act as a wake-up call of your drive, internal compass, and commitment to the world. You'll make a vocational venture that reverberates with profundity and satisfaction by utilizing insightful readiness, continuous headway, and a commitment to leaving a decent imprint. We should begin the way to laying out a dependable and significant vocation, where each step is a stroke in the work of art that is your expert memoir.

Chapter 12

Compelling Relational abilities:

Uniting Individuals in the Work Environment

Connection is more important than just words in communication. This part examines the art of communication by examining both the spoken and nonverbal cues that lay the groundwork for every productive exchange. Building relationships, motivating action, and promoting understanding are equally as important as disseminating information.

The Dance of Association in Verbal and Non-Verbal Correspondence

Envision a discussion where every articulation, motion, and word cooperates to wind around a trap of significance. Understanding the significance of both verbal and nonverbal correspondence is the focal point of this part. Your manner of speaking, the glimmer in your eye, and the developments you use to accentuate your message all matter. We'll take a gander at how to facilitate your verbal and nonverbal signals to convey messages that are significant, clear, and true.
Imagine the depth of connection that will occur when your words and body language are in perfect unison and resonate deeply with the individuals you engage with.

Compassionate Tuning in The Backbone of Significant Associations

Communication is a two-way street, and the unsung hero of every conversation is the one who is listening. This part is an invitation to listen, not simply to hear, to comprehend, empathize, and validate. We'll look at techniques for attentive listening so you can focus on the words themselves as well as the feelings and intentions behind them. It involves making a place where other people feel respected and heard.

Consider the impacts of causing others to feel seen and figured out in discussions by being truly present.

Getting comfortable with Yourself and True Self-Articulation

In the realm of communication, your voice is like your digital fingerprint. Discovering and claiming your communication style is the focus of this section. Whether you're speaking to a group of people, a client, or a coworker, it's important to express yourself in a way that feels genuine to who you are. We'll look at methods for developing your authentic voice, expressing yourself clearly, and delivering your message in a way that makes an impact.

Envision the conviction and confirmation you will radiate when you talk from the heart, offering your viewpoints and perspectives with truthfulness and a feeling of direction

Step-by-step instructions to Have Intense Discussions and Do It With Empathy and Boldness

Having difficult dialogues is not a barrier; rather, it is a chance for understanding and growth. This section discusses how to handle delicate subjects with empathy. Finding common ground, looking for solutions, and upholding respect even when you disagree are all important. We'll look at techniques for handling these discussions sensitively and tactfully so that they result in fruitful solutions.

Imagine the trust and respect that will grow as a result of managing challenging talks with a mix of compassion and boldness.

Business Persuasive Communication: Motivating Action and Alignment

Correspondence is something beyond trading data; it likewise includes spurring others to make a move and advancing arrangements around a typical goal. The craft of influence is shrouded in this part. It includes creating convincing correspondences, rousing inspiration, and resulting in huge impacts. We'll take a gander at techniques for sorting out convincing contentions, changing informing to your crowd, and impacting others through story.

Consider the impact of your words as they spur others to make a move and unite individuals for a common reason as well as illuminating them.

You'll be a master of connection by the time you finish this course, not just a set of communication skills. You'll develop relationships that go beyond business dealings and create a professional network based on trust and understanding through authentic expression, sympathetic listening, and persuasive communication. Let's begin this road of mastering communication, where each interaction is a chance to build relationships between people on a professional level.

Chapter 13

The Drawn-out Advantages of Relationship Authority in Your Profession:

Cultivating Connections Past Exchanges

Connections aren't simply strings in the enormous embroidery of your work; they're the bright, entwining strands that make the central construction of your profession way. The effect that genuine, significant associations can have on your vocation direction is heartfeltly investigated in this part.

Changing Exchanges into Groundbreaking Encounters: The Force of Real Association

Consider your transactions as any open doors to really interface — to appreciate, to empower, and to move — instead of just trading words. This part examines how to foster associations that go past transactions and make each connection an opportunity to fashion enduring bonds. It's tied in with genuinely communicating with others, showing that you care about their prosperity and prosperity.

Envision the profundity of unwavering trust that will develop through associations in light of truthfulness and regard for each other.

Compassionate Tuning in The Backbone of Significant Associations

Talking is just a single piece of correspondence; the other is tuning in with a receptive outlook. This part is a challenge to tune in, not just to hear, grasp, sympathize, and approve. It's tied in with laying out a climate where individuals feel appreciated and heard, where their perspectives and encounters are thought about.

Envision the profundity of association that outcomes from real tuning in, making associations that go past the surface.

The Force of Help and Mentorship to Engage Others

Your process isn't just about you improving; it's likewise about the impact you have on others' turn of events and achievement. Being a wellspring of consolation, motivation, and tutoring is the focal point of this part. It includes seeing likely in people around you and effectively aiding their development. Through your initiative, you rise above the job of a straightforward collaborator to turn into an image of freedom.

Envision the fulfillment and pride you will feel as individuals you have helped all through their ways to develop and succeed.

Regulating Difficulties Together: Making Associations in Hardship

Issues aren't limits; they're valuable and open doors for a more significant bond and shared improvement. This part discusses overcoming hindrances close to your master neighborhood. It's connected to giving and getting support, collaborating to deal with issues, and arising on the contrary side of trouble with ties that are more grounded than at some other time

Envision the strength and concordance that would rise out of a local where individuals cooperate to conquer obstructions since they are certain they can do such as a solitary, strong power.

Local area Achievement Festivity: Perceiving Aggregate Achievement

Achievement is a common festival as opposed to an individual accomplishment. You are urged to perceive and commend your achievements as well as the victories of your expert local area in this segment. It includes acknowledging how firmly connected your prosperity is to that of people around you and praising their accomplishments as though they were your own.

Envision the soul of collaboration and regard that will encompass each common triumph.

You won't just fathom the impacts of relationship dominance toward the finish of this part; you will likewise have experienced them. You'll construct an expert local area that goes past transactions and turns into a wellspring of persevering through motivation and development using certifiable association, empathic tuning in, and a devotion to empowering and supporting others. We should set out on this street of relationship authority, where every cooperation offers the opportunity to cultivate ties that will endure and add to the texture of your expert heritage.

Conclusion

We expect the boundless potential that is hanging tight for you as we close the end drape on this examination of the Companion Impact Outline. "Raise Your Profession" is something other than a how-to manual; it's likewise a lifestyle, a source of inspiration, and a commitment to progress.

You are currently ready to effectively and legitimately arrange the mind-boggling dance of expert connections on account of the experiences you have acquired from these pages. You have the right stuff important to make associations that depend on regard and shared goals that are both expansive and durable.

Remember that you are something beyond an individual when you enter the powerful universe of your vocation: you are a center of potential and impact. Each cooperation, trade of thoughts, and collaboration can modify your direction and have an enduring effect on the world.

With enthusiasm, embrace this new information since even the longest excursion begins with a solitary step. Foster your organization with reason, develop associations that are significant to you, and perceive what you mean for spreads a long way past the extent of your current ventures.

You are in good company as you continue looking for proficient accomplishment, remember that. Your fantasies will remain steadfast on the mainstays of the connections you develop. They act as the establishment for your excursion, the nourishment for your turn of events, and the heritage you abandon.

You are furnished with the Companion Impact Diagram, a compass that will lead you through the unseen waters of your calling, so go out, my peruser, with certainty and conviction. Raise yourself as well as the people around you since, in the realm of profound associations, the gathering is more remarkable than the person.

This isn't the end, however, it is the start of another section where the power you hold and the associations you construct can shape an example of overcoming adversity that is exceptionally yours. Acknowledge it, live it, and let it take you to incomprehensible levels. Your process has recently begun.

Consider the huge effect that looks for you as you approach this changing excursion. The Companion Impact Outline is more than just a rundown of proposals; an idea could change how you live and work.

Recall the strength that lives in these encounters as you spread out new affiliations, support existing associations, and partake in agreeable exercises. Each might potentially be a blaze that gets the fires going of creativity and accomplishment, going probably as an improvement gas pedal.

You presently have a tool stash that goes past the limits of the standard way of thinking to mesh into the huge embroidery of your expert story. You can lay out ties that go past clear transactions, winding around a huge organization of impact.

Perceiving the significance of human association in the journey of greatness is an extravagance, hence embracing this newly discovered understanding with appreciation. Your organization is a genuine, breathing living being that can progress your profession as well as the goals of everybody in your nearby area. It isn't simply a rundown of names and positions.

Recollect that every association, discussion, and cooperation might potentially be a pivotal turning point as you proceed. They structure the foundation of your instance of conquering affliction and will be woven with reason, reliability, and objectivity.b

This is your encouragement to enter the universe of expert improvement with certainty and the information on the Companion Impact Outline. Permit it to lead you, persuade you, and convey you to levels you might not have recently imagined. Dear peruser, your process is an embroidery standing by to be wound around, and you hold the strings of association and impact. Acknowledge them and permit them to push you to significance.